T0129480

THE
GRAD STUDENT'S GUIDE
TO KANT'S CRITIQUE
OF PURE REASON

THE
GRAD STUDENT'S GUIDE
TO KANT'S CRITIQUE
OF PURE REASON

JOSEPH W. LONG

THE GRAD STUDENT'S GUIDE TO
KANT'S CRITIQUE OF PURE REASON

iUniverse books may be ordered through booksellers or by contacting:

iUniverse
1663 Liberty Drive
Bloomington, IN 47403
www.iuniverse.com
1-800-Authors (1-800-288-4677)

Because of the dynamic nature of the Internet, any web addresses or links contained in this book may have changed since publication and may no longer be valid. The views expressed in this work are solely those of the author and do not necessarily reflect the views of the publisher, and the publisher hereby disclaims any responsibility for them.

Any people depicted in stock imagery provided by Thinkstock are models, and such images are being used for illustrative purposes only. Certain stock imagery © Thinkstock.

ISBN: 978-1-5320-0403-2 (sc)
ISBN: 978-1-5320-0404-9 (e)

Library of Congress Control Number: 2016912803

Print information available on the last page.

iUniverse rev. date: 10/25/2016

CONTENTS

ACKNOWLEDGMENTS

This work would not be possible without the contributions of many colleagues, professors, students, and friends. I am deeply indebted to Professor William Charron, whose graduate seminar on Kant's first critique provided both the groundwork for this study guide and the inspiration for its publication. I also wish to thank Professors Manfred Kuehn, Charlene Haddock Seigfried, Jan Cover, and William McBride for their guidance and inspiration. I owe a debt of thanks to my colleagues Professors John Tilley, Jason Eberl, and Randy Jensen for stimulating conversations about Kant's philosophy.

In particular, I would like to acknowledge the gracious mentorship of the late Professor William L. Rowe (1931–2015), whose life and work exemplified the sovereign nature of reason.

INTRODUCTION

The *Critique of Pure Reason* (commonly known within the field of philosophy as Kant's "first critique," as it precedes his *Critique of Practical Reason* and *Critique of Judgment*) was first published in 1781, with a second edition following in 1787. It is the paramount philosophical publication of the Enlightenment and one of the most important and influential works in the history of Western thought.

It is also one of the cardinal texts for students of philosophy at both the graduate and undergraduate levels. Any PhD candidate taking her prelim exams in the history of philosophy can expect a hearty array of questions about the *Critique of Pure Reason*. And any graduate student interested in metaphysics or epistemology would do himself a great disservice if he failed to take a seminar on Kant's seminal work.

My own prelim exam in the history of modern and contemporary philosophy featured eight essay questions. Three of those were about Kant's first critique. During my first faculty interviews at the American Philosophical Association meetings, several of my prospective employers asked me questions about Kant simply to gauge my understanding of his philosophy and its historical context.

And as a professor and instructor at Purdue University, Northwestern College, University of St. Thomas, and IUPUI, I have continued to emphasize the importance of Kant's metaphysics and epistemology.

I think graduate students in philosophy should find this little guide helpful. But this book is not intended exclusively for grad students. I hope it will serve as a valuable resource for undergraduates, teaching assistants, professors and other scholars, as well as those individuals outside of academia who have a general interest in Kant's philosophy.

The *Critique of Pure Reason* has gained a reputation as a brilliant but inaccessible philosophical treatise, an unreadable masterpiece. While it's true that the *Critique* is dense, ungainly in style, and intimidating to the uninitiated, it is not inaccessible to the careful student. Of course, a guide can be extremely helpful. That's why this book is here.

The primary aim of the first critique is to explore the scope and limits of pure reason. It is, in fact, a critical examination of reason by reason.

It is, likewise, an inquiry into the possibility of metaphysics. Ultimately, Kant concludes that we cannot know complete metaphysical truth via pure reason as the continental rationalists claim. The noumenal world, out there external to our minds, is inaccessible to us. But the British empiricists miss the mark as well. There are important truths, for instance, universal mathematical and scientific truths, that we can know via pure reason. This is because it is possible to know certain synthetic a priori judgments. Kant's synthesis of rationalism and empiricism is but one of the revolutionary turns in the *Critique of Pure Reason*.

Another revolutionary turn comes in Kant's idealist view of time and space. According to Kant, time and space are not objectively real but rather a framework within which our experiences are constructed. It is, in large part, this framework of time and space that makes our sensory experiences possible, or at least meaningful. This view has momentous (perhaps even alarming) implications for our traditional notion of causality. Given Kant's view, if Y follows X (or if indeed we say that X causes Y), it is because our minds arrange it so. The mind is not a tabula rasa but rather an active shaper and creator of one's experiences.

Finally, Kant's first critique is revolutionary because it redefines the role of metaphysics as a critique of pure reason and thus shifts the focus of philosophy from investigating the world as such to investigating the way in which we process and shape our experience of the world.

It is doubtful that any single volume (and certainly not this brief guide) could provide an adequately detailed explication of the full sum of Kant's first critique, but in this guide, I will attempt to make plain many of the most salient, most seminal, and most obdurate of the *Critique's* concepts and arguments.

In part 1 of this book, I will provide definitions for key terms that students of Kant's first critique will need to understand. In particular, I will explain what Kant means by the terms *analytic* and *synthetic* and *a priori* and *a posteriori*, and I will explain the nature and role of synthetic a priori judgments, which are essential to Kant's philosophy. Next, I will discuss his notion of experience, some of its important components—including sensations, intuitions, and concepts—and explain how Kant believes that our manifold of subjective appearances can be transformed into an objectively valid experience. I will conclude part 1 with a brief explication of Kant's philosophical worldview, transcendental idealism, as well as his transcendental proof, the conditions for the possibility of geometry, and his so-called *first antinomy*.

In part 2, I will briefly retreat to examine the historical setting of the problem at the heart of the critique of pure reason. I will also attempt to provide a terse but lucid treatment of Kant's categories of the understanding, forms of judgment, principles of pure understanding, logic, regulative and constituitive judgments, experience, and metaphysics. Finally, I will conclude part 2 with Kant's critical refutation of skepticism, idealism, and dogmatic rationalism.

In an effort to provide the most valuable rudder through the deep waters of Kant's magnum opus, I have worked very close to the text and quoted many passages that students should find helpful. Readers should note that all references to Kant's text come from the Norman Kemp Smith translation (New York: St. Martin's, 1929), and I have included both A and B page numbers where applicable. A and B numbers are traditionally used in Kant scholarship to indicate the page numbers in both the A (1781) and B (1787) editions.

PART 1

In part 1 of this book, I will reconstruct some of the main arguments of Kant's first critique, explaining how the manifold of subjective appearances can be transformed into a unified and objectively valid experience. I will explain Kant's own philosophical weltanschauung, transcendental idealism. This discussion will include his transcendental proof, the transcendental conditions for the possibility of geometry, and his first antinomy, each of which will give us a distinct argument for transcendental idealism. But first, I should explore what Kant means by a critique of pure reason and define its relationship to transcendental philosophy and synthetic a priori judgments.

I

CRITIQUING PURE REASON

The question *What does Kant mean by a critique of pure reason?* can be broken down into four smaller and more manageable questions: What is pure reason? What sort of critique is Kant making? What does Kant mean by metaphysics and how is it related to the critique of pure reason? What are synthetic a priori judgments and what is their importance to the critique of pure reason?

a. What is pure reason?

Kant uses the term *pure reason* to mean rational thought wholly independent and wholly purged of all things empirical and sensational. He writes, pure reason is "the faculty of reason in general ... *independently of all experience.*"[1] And: reason is "pure when there is no admixture of anything empirical."[2] And again: reason is pure "when all the material

---

[1] Immanuel Kant, *Critique of Pure Reason,* trans. Norman Kemp Smith (New York: St. Martin's, 1929, copyright 1781), Axii; see also Axviii.

[2] Ibid., B3.

and assistance of experience are taken away …"[3] And finally, pure reason is what we can know "absolutely *a priori*."[4]

b. What sort of critique is Kant making?

The critique of pure reason is described by Kant as a "special science" that examines the "sources and limits" of pure reason.[5] It is appropriately called a *critique* because it merely examines, clarifies, and corrects reason; it does not hope to extend its powers or to develop it into something more.[6] Kant further calls the critique of pure reason a "tribunal which will assure to reason its lawful claims, and dismiss all groundless pretensions …"[7] and which will settle "all disputes of pure reason."[8] The critique is guided by five

---

[3] Ibid., Axiv.

[4] In the first edition (only) of the *Critique of Pure Reason*, Kant distinguishes *pure knowledge* from *absolutely pure knowledge*. He writes, "Any knowledge is entitled pure, if it be not mixed with anything extraneous. But knowledge is more particularly to be called absolutely pure, if no experience or sensation whatsoever be mingled with it, and if it be therefore possible completely *a priori*" (A11). This distinction would seem to suggest that simply pure reason is not entirely pure, because it is less pure than absolutely pure reason, and thus complicates the notion of pure reason. (This may be the reason it was omitted from the second edition.) However, this distinction need not make the term *pure reason* problematic for our purposes in this book. Herein, I will use the term *pure* as Kant uses it throughout the majority of his work.

[5] Ibid., A11/B24–25.

[6] Ibid., A11–12/B25–26.

[7] Ibid., Axii.

[8] Ibid., A751/B779.

important requirements of reason. These are completeness, exhaustiveness, certainty, clarity,[9] and freedom. Kant stresses this last requirement in several passages: "Reason depends on ... freedom for its very existence. For reason has no dictatorial authority; its verdict is always simply the agreement of free citizens, of whom each one must be permitted to express, without let or hindrance, his objections or even his veto."[10] Again: reason must remain free from "despotic decrees."[11] So the critique of pure reason is a complete, exhaustive, certain, clear, and free self-examination of reason by reason.

Kant believes that such a critique is necessary for two reasons. First, if reason is not critical of itself, its nature, sources, and limits, then it becomes dogmatic. In fact, Kant defines *dogmatism* as the "procedure of pure reason, *without previous examination of its powers*."[12] Further, he states, even if reason is not dogmatic, limiting criticism will leave it open to the charge of dogmatism. He writes, if reason limits "criticism by any prohibitions, it must harm itself, drawing upon itself a damaging suspicion."[13] Second, the critique is necessary because only through such an examination can we learn whether the propositions concerning transcendent metaphysics are knowable. He writes, "The critique of pure reason will contain all that is essential in transcendental

---

[9] Ibid., Axv.

[10] Ibid., A738–739/B766–767.

[11] Ibid., Axii; see also A752/B780.

[12] Ibid., Bxxxv.

[13] Ibid., A738/B766.

philosophy."[14] To understand this connection between the critique of pure reason and metaphysics, we must first examine what Kant means by metaphysics, or transcendental philosophy.

c. What does Kant mean by metaphysics, and how is it related to the critique of pure reason?

Although Kant will ultimately say that the propositions concerning transcendent philosophy are not *knowable* but legitimately accessible through faith,[15] he does not denigrate metaphysical questions or rule them out of court. Rather, he recognizes their importance, calling metaphysics "fundamental,"[16] "unavoidable,"[17] and "indispensable to human reason."[18] He adds that it is "a science whose every branch may be cut away but whose root cannot be destroyed."[19] There are, however, significant problems limiting metaphysics' success as a science. As Kant says, "the students of metaphysics [have not exhibited] any kind of unanimity in their contentions."[20] This, he continues, "shows ... that the procedure of metaphysics has hitherto been a merely random groping ... of mere concepts."[21] The

---

[14] Ibid., A14/B28.
[15] Ibid., A745/B773; A753/B781; A741/B769; Bxix–xx.
[16] Ibid., Bxxiv.
[17] Ibid., A3/B7.
[18] Ibid., B24.
[19] Ibid., B24.
[20] Ibid., Bxv.
[21] Ibid., Bxv.

lack of unanimity of its claims along with the uncertainty of its methodology lead Kant to call transcendent philosophy a "battle-field of ... endless controversies."[22]

The principal problems of metaphysics are enumerated by Kant as "*God, freedom,* and *immortality.*"[23] These problems and their would-be solutions *transcend* all possible human experience.[24] As I will show, this will be problematic to the justification of metaphysics and will ultimately be part of the downfall of metaphysics as a successful science. But before we can see why, we must understand what Kant calls *synthetic a priori* judgments and recognize their importance to metaphysics and the critique of pure reason.

d. What are synthetic a priori judgments, and what is their importance to the critique of pure reason?

Judgments, in general, are important for Kant because he holds that all knowledge is discursive.[25] He writes, "we can reduce all acts of the understanding to judgments."[26] Judgments are essentially the "functions of unity among our representations."[27] Kant says that the principles of metaphysics must be synthetic a priori judgments. To understand what he means by this, we have to explore his

---

[22] Ibid., Aviii.

[23] Ibid., A3/B7.

[24] Ibid., Bxix–xx.

[25] Ibid., A68/B93.

[26] Ibid., A69/B94.

[27] Ibid., A69/B93.

distinctions between analytic and synthetic judgments and
between a priori and a posteriori judgments.

Kant writes, "Either the predicate B belongs to the
subject A, as something which is (covertly) contained in
this concept A; or B lies outside the concept A, although it
does indeed stand in connection with it."[28] The former is
a case of what Kant calls an *analytic* judgment; the latter,
a *synthetic* one. Analytic judgments are "those in which
the connection of the predicate with the subject is thought
through identity ..."[29] To say it another way, the predicate of
an analytic judgment adds nothing to the subject. Analytic
judgments are important, Kant says, but only for the
clearness of concepts.[30]

Conversely, all judgments that extend beyond the mere
concept of the subject and add something new to it are
synthetic.[31] There is no connection of identity between
the subject and predicate of synthetic judgments.[32] Kant
writes, synthetic judgments "pass beyond our concept of
the object."[33] And again: "there is not to be found a single
synthetic judgment directly derived from concepts."[34] All
judgments of experience are of this type.[35]

[28] Ibid., A6/B10.
[29] Ibid., A7/B10–11.
[30] Ibid., A10/B14.
[31] Ibid., A7/B11.
[32] Ibid., A7/B10–11.
[33] Ibid., A765/B793.
[34] Ibid., A736/B764.
[35] Ibid., A7/B11.

Kant provides us with a test for determining whether judgments are analytic or synthetic. If the denial of the judgment would constitute a contradiction, then the judgment is analytic. If, however, there would be no contradiction, the judgment is synthetic. He writes, "*The principle of contradiction* must therefore be recognized as being the universal and completely sufficient *principle of all analytic knowledge*."[36]

The analytic/synthetic distinction can be called a logico-semantic distinction in that it is formal and concerns concepts. The a priori / a posteriori distinction, on the other hand, (as Kant here uses the terms),[37] is not concerned with logic or the semantic meaning of judgments but rather with their justification. Thus, we can call this an epistemological distinction. An a priori judgment is a clear and certain judgment[38] that cannot be justified by any empirical evidence.[39] Further, a priori judgments are necessary and strictly universal, or lie beyond all possible experience as metaphysical judgments do. As to the necessity and universality of a priori judgments, Kant writes as follows: "Any knowledge that professes to hold *a priori* lays claim to be regarded as absolutely necessary."[40] "[*A*

---

[36] Ibid., A151/B191.

[37] Kant's use of the term *a priori* does not consistently refer to the way in which a judgment is *justified*. He also uses the term to point to the *origin* of a particular concept, intuition, judgment, or idea. I discuss this in more detail in the section on concepts and intuitions.

[38] *Critique of Pure Reason*, A2.

[39] Ibid., B3.

[40] Ibid., Axv.

priori knowledge gives] to assertions true universality and strict necessity, such as mere empirical knowledge cannot supply."[41] Further, universality and necessity always go together, so that if we know a claim to be necessary, we can also know it to be universal, and vice versa: "Necessity and strict universality are thus sure criteria of *a priori* knowledge, and are inseparable from one another."[42]

On the contrary, an empirical or a posteriori judgment is any judgment that can be justified by experiential or sensational evidence. We can know such judgments to be true but not to be strictly necessary or universal: "Experience tells us, indeed, what is, but not that it must necessarily be so, and not otherwise. It therefore gives no true universality."[43] All empirical judgments can be supported by experiential means, such as measurement or observation.

It is easy to see how we can hold and justify judgments that are both analytic and a priori. Such a proposition as "All bachelors are men" is an analytic a priori judgment. The predicate, *men,* is contained (covertly) in the concept of the subject, *bachelors.* Further, we do not need any sensory evidence to justify this statement. We can also see prima facie that synthetic empirical statements are not difficult to justify. "A Bengal tiger has thirty teeth" would be an example of a judgment that is both synthetic and empirical. The predicate, *having thirty teeth,* is not entailed in the subject, *a Bengal tiger*; nor is it strictly universal or necessary,

---

[41] Ibid., A2.

[42] Ibid., B4.

[43] Ibid., A2; see also B3.

although it might very well be true. Our justification for such a statement would have to come through empirical means, probably by counting the number of teeth in a large number of Bengal tigers and then making an inductive inference about all Bengals.

There seem, however, to be some judgments that are both synthetic and a priori. The principles of metaphysics, Kant says, must be so, because they would have to reach beyond mere concepts (be synthetic) and also be strictly necessary and universal (a priori.) Other synthetic a priori judgments would include the principles of mathematics, the principles of natural science, the principles of morality, and the principles of aesthetics. Since these principles are so important, it is also urgent that we be able to justify them. However, the means of their justification is not intuitively apparent. So the critical question of the critique of pure reason is, how are synthetic a priori judgments possible? (How are they justified?)

II

Experience

Kant eventually resolves the crucial problem of the justification of synthetic a priori judgments through transcendental idealism. Before we can understand this worldview, however, we must come to understand some of his more basic notions, particularly the notion of experience and its components. In this section, I will offer a basic picture of what Kant means by sensations, intuitions and concepts, and appearances and experience, and I will show how Kant reasons that appearances can be transformed into an empirically real experience.

a. Sensations

Sensation is the instantaneous and wholly empirical "matter of perception."[44] Kant writes, sensation is the "element in the appearances (... the matter of perception) which can never be known *a priori*." He continues, in the same section, saying, "Apprehension by means merely of sensation

---

[44] Ibid., A167/B209.

occupies only an instant ..."[45] Elsewhere, he defines sensation as "The effect of an object upon the faculty of representation ..."[46] These sensations have intensive but not extensive magnitudes.[47] This means they have various intensities—for instance, intensities of sight or sound but not spatiotemporal intensities. For example, we may have a sensation of a red object, but this sensation is not contained in space or time. Space and time, we will find, are a priori representations. Further, sensations, by themselves, have no objective validity, or as Kant writes, they are not in themselves "objective representation[s],"[48] but, as we will soon see, they are still a vital part of our empirically real experience.

b. Intuitions and Concepts

Intuitions and concepts are two vital parts of experience for Kant, and they are intimately connected to each other. He writes, "Now there are two conditions under which alone the knowledge of an object is possible, first *intuition,* through which it is given, though only as appearance; secondly, *concept,* through which an object is thought corresponding

---

[45] Ibid., A167/B209.

[46] Ibid., A20/B34.

[47] Ibid., A166/B209. While sensations are wholly empirical, the fact that they have magnitudes is known a priori. Kant writes, "... though all sensations as such are given only *a posteriori,* their property of possessing a degree can be known *a priori*" (A176/B218).

[48] Ibid., A166/B209.

to this intuition."[49] I will begin by discussing what Kant means by intuitions and then move on to concepts.

At the beginning of the Transcendental Aesthetic, Kant writes, "In whatever manner and by whatever means a mode of knowledge may relate to objects, *intuition* is that through which it is in immediate relation to them, and to which all thought as a means is directed."[50] He continues, "Objects are *given* to us by means of sensibility, and it alone yields us *intuitions* …"[51] There are two types of intuitions. These are pure (or a priori[52]) and empirical. The type (discussed above) that is directly related to sensibility is empirical intuition. Kant writes, "That intuition which is in relation to the object through sensation is entitled empirical."[53] We should begin, however, with pure intuitions, because these are necessary for the achievement of empirical intuitions.

"The only intuition that is given *a priori*," Kant writes, "is that of the mere form of appearances, space and time."[54] He refers to these pure intuitions elsewhere, as the "two original *quanta* of all our intuition."[55] That time and space are intuitions does not mean that they are unreal. For Kant, neither time nor space can be said to be "things

---

[49] Ibid., A92/B125.

[50] Ibid., A19/B33.

[51] Ibid., A19/B33.

[52] By *a priori,* Kant here means that the *origin* of the intuition is internal and not a product of sensibility. This is contrasted to his earlier use of the word, where *a priori* meant that it could not be *justified* by any empirical means; see footnote 37.

[53] Ibid., A20/B34.

[54] Ibid., A720/B748.

[55] Ibid., A411/B438.

in themselves …"[56]; however, both are empirically real.[57] They are not empirical concepts, nor are they "derived from outer experiences,"[58] but they are the *forms* of outer sense, and as such are necessary a priori representations, and so have empirical reality, though transcendental ideality. Kant writes, "Our exposition therefore establishes the *reality,* that is, the objective validity, of space [and also time][59] in respect of whatever can be presented to us outwardly as object, but also at the same time the *ideality* of space in respect of things when they are considered in themselves through reason …"[60]

It is with the aid of these pure intuitions, space and time, that empirical intuitions are possible. In fact, empirical intuitions are created through the synthesis of sensations with pure intuitions in the imagination. The perception of objects in motion through space and time relies on this synthesis. Kant writes:

> Psychologists have hitherto failed to realise that imagination is a necessary ingredient of perception itself. This is due partly to the fact that the faculty has been limited to reproduction, partly to the belief that the senses not only supply impressions but also combine

---

[56] Ibid., A26/B42; A28/B44; A33/B49.

[57] Ibid., A28/B44; A35/B52.

[58] Ibid., A23/B38; A30/B46.

[59] Ibid., A35–36/B52. In this passage, Kant reaches the same conclusions for time as he does earlier for space.

[60] Ibid., A28/B44.

them so as to generate images of objects. For that purpose something more than the mere receptivity of impressions is undoubtedly required, namely, a function for the synthesis of them.[61]

Specifically, the synthesis of the manifold of immediate sensations with the pure intuitions of space and time and the imaginative ability to construct a line through space and time[62] brings subjective unity to empirical intuitions. The objects of these intuitions are appearances: "The undetermined object of an empirical intuition is entitled *appearance*."[63] Before embarking on a discussion of appearances and the problem of transforming appearances into experiences, I should briefly discuss Kant's notion of concepts, which is related to his notion of intuitions.

"[B]esides intuition," Kant writes, "there is no other mode of knowledge except by means of concepts."[64] A concept is that "through which an object is thought corresponding to … intuition."[65] It is thought "through understanding, and from the understanding arise *concepts*."[66] It is sometimes difficult to differentiate concepts from intuitions. Kant cites the example of mathematics, which is intuitional but may appear to be merely conceptual: the fact that mathematics is

[61] Ibid., A121n.
[62] Ibid., B137–138, 154–156.
[63] Ibid., A20/B34.
[64] Ibid., A68/B92–93.
[65] Ibid., A92/B125.
[66] Ibid., A19/B33.

intuitional "is easily overlooked, since this intuition can itself be given *a priori,* and is therefore hardly to be distinguished from a bare and pure concept."[67] Nevertheless, concepts are distinct from intuitions. He writes:

> Whereas all intuitions, as sensible, rest on affections, concepts rest on functions. By 'function' I mean the unity of the act of bringing various representations under one common representation. Concepts are based on the spontaneity of thought, sensible intuitions on the receptivity of impressions.[68]

Like intuitions, concepts can be pure (a priori[69]) or empirical. A pure concept is a synthesis of an entirely a priori manifold.[70] If the manifold contains experiential data from sensations, then the synthesis and the concept are *empirical.* Kant's goal in the Analytic of Concepts is to find all the pure concepts of synthesis, which are the logical forms of judgments, or the categories.[71] The logical forms are incapable of explanation but can be known completely a priori *and are a necessary condition for experience.* Kant writes, "There is something strange and even absurd in the assertion that there should be a concept which possesses

---

[67] Ibid., A4/B8.

[68] Ibid., A68/B93.

[69] By *a priori,* Kant once again is referring to the origin and not the justification of a concept; see footnotes 37 and 52.

[70] Ibid., A77/B103.

[71] Ibid., A80/B106.

a meaning and yet is not capable of any explanation. But the categories have this particular feature ..."[72] These he asserts and lists in the table of categories. There are four categories—quantity, quality, relation, and modality—and three types of judgment within each general category as follows:[73]

Quantity	Quality	Relation	Modality
universal	affirmative	categorical	problematic
particular	negative	hypothetical	assertoric
singular	infinite	disjunctive	apodeictic

c. Appearances and Experience

Kant differentiates things-in-themselves (or the ontological reality of things external to minds) from things-as-appearances.[74] The appearance / reality distinction is not new with Kant. In fact, philosophers since Plato have worried about *saving the appearances* and hooking them up to things-in-themselves. Appearances have *subjective* unity.[75] They are the collective objects of empirical intuitions[76] and are combined with consciousness to create perception.[77] What Kant aims to do in his effort to *save the appearances*

---

[72] Ibid., A244/B302.

[73] For a discussion of the categories themselves, see A70–84/B95–116.

[74] Ibid., Bxxin.

[75] Ibid., A155–156/B195–196.

[76] Ibid., A20/B34.

[77] Ibid., A120.

is to take the subjective unity of appearances and transform them into experience, which will have *objective* unity and objective validity, that is to say, be empirically real.

Sensations, intuitions, concepts, and appearances are all necessary elements of experience. Sensations synthesized with pure intuitions yield empirical intuitions.[78] An object thought through understanding[79] corresponding to intuitions[80] is a concept. Pure concepts, the categories, are necessary for the possibility of experience. Finally, appearances are synthesized in understanding into a single and objectively real experience.[81] Kant writes, "Experience … rests on the synthetic unity of appearances, that is, on a synthesis according to concepts of an object of appearances in general. Apart from such synthesis it would not be knowledge …"[82] Again: "Experience is an empirical knowledge, that is, a knowledge which determines an object through perceptions. It is a synthesis of perceptions, not contained in perception but itself containing in one consciousness the synthetic unity of the manifold of perceptions."[83]

In this single synthesis, Kant has achieved two important goals. He has found a way to save things-as-appearances by synthesizing them into empirically real, objectively valid, intersubjective experiences, and he has found a way of synthesizing synthetic elements, such as sensations and

---

[78] Ibid., A121; A20/B34.

[79] Ibid., A19/B33.

[80] Ibid., A92/B125.

[81] Ibid., A177/B218.

[82] Ibid., A156/B195.

[83] Ibid., A176/B218.

appearances, together with a priori elements, such as pure intuitions and the pure concepts, the categories. Together in experience, they can constitute synthetic a priori judgments, and, Kant writes, "Apart from this relation synthetic *a priori* principles are completely impossible."[84] The project is not yet finished, however. First, he must explain how the synthetic a priori principles of experience are justified through a transcendental proof. But before we consider this proof, I wish to explain his philosophical weltanschauung, transcendental idealism.

---

[84] Ibid., A157/B196.

III

TRANSCENDENTAL
IDEALISM AND PROOFS

In this section, I hope to explain Kant's ontological and epistemological worldview, *transcendental idealism*. I will also explain what he means by a transcendental proof and present the first of his three arguments for transcendental idealism. Next, I will explain his transcendental conditions for the possibility of geometry and present his second argument for transcendental idealism. Finally, I will explain Kant's so-called *first antinomy* together with its solution and present his third argument for transcendental idealism. I should begin, however, by spelling out what he means by this crucial doctrine.

a. Transcendental Idealism

In section II-c, I showed how Kant found it possible to save the appearances by transforming them into a single, objectively valid experience. In this section, I want to discuss further what this means. Kant has not eliminated the gap between mind-independent objects and mental representations of objects in such a way as to offer a sort of ontological realism about these objects. This is not his aim; nor, in fact, does he think this is possible. Rather, appearances are saved because all objects in space and time are merely mental representations and do not, themselves, have existence external to minds. Kant writes:

> [A]ll objects of any experience possible to us are nothing but appearances, that is, mere representations, which, in the manner in which they are represented, as extended beings, or as a series of alterations, have no independent existence outside our thoughts. This doctrine I entitle *transcendental idealism*. The realist in the transcendental meaning of this term, treats these modifications of our sensibility as self-subsistent things, that is, treats *mere representations* as things in themselves.[85]

Kant's point here is difficult to grasp. It may seem from this passage that he is denying that the objects of our experience are in any sense *real*. However, he wants to maintain that although they are transcendentally ideal, they are still empirically real:

> Our transcendental idealism, on the contrary, admits the reality of the objects of outer intuition, as intuited in space, and of all

---

[85] Ibid., A491/B519.

changes in time, as represented by inner sense. For since space is a form of that intuition which we entitle outer, and since without objects in space there would be no empirical representation whatsoever, we can and must regard the extended beings in it as real; and the same is true of time.[86]

b. Transcendental Proof

Kant's conception of transcendental proof is instrumental to his view of transcendental idealism. He argues that synthetic a priori principles give us the necessary conditions for experience only given the transcendental ideality of objects in space.[87] This point will become clearer when we examine the first of Kant's three arguments for transcendental idealism, which comes via a transcendental deduction or transcendental proof. Before giving the argument though, let me first explain what a transcendental proof is. Transcendental proofs argue backward, in a sense, from an established conclusion to a necessary premise in the argument that produces that conclusion. Kant writes, "The proof proceeds by showing that experience itself, and therefore the object of experience, would be impossible without a connection of this kind." He continues: "Accordingly, the proof must also at the same time show the possibility of

---

[86] Ibid., A491–492/B520.

[87] Kant argues this point in: Immanuel Kant, *Prolegomena to Any Future Metaphysics*, trans. Paul Carus, revised by James W. Ellington (Indianapolis: Hackett, 1985, copyright 1783), 318–319.

arriving synthetically and *a priori* at some knowledge of things which was not contained in the concepts of them."[88]

Kant, further, sets out three rules regarding transcendental proofs, which I will enumerate here in full:

1. The first rule is ... not to attempt any transcendental proofs until we have considered, with a view to obtaining justification for them, from what source we propose to derive the principles on which the proofs are to be based, and with what right we may expect success in our inferences.[89]

2. The second peculiarity of transcendental proofs is that only *one* proof can be found for each transcendental proposition. If I am inferring not from concepts but from the intuition which corresponds to a concept, be it a pure intuition as in mathematics, or an empirical intuition as in natural science, the intuition which serves as the basis of the inference supplies me with manifold material for synthetic propositions, material which I can connect in more than one way, so that, as it is permissible for me to start from more

[88] *Critique of Pure Reason,* A783/B811.
[89] Ibid., A786/B814.

than one point, I can arrive at the same proposition by different paths.[90]

3. The third rule ... is that its proofs must never be *apogogical,* but always *ostensive.* The direct or ostensive proof, in every kind of knowledge, is that which combines with the conviction of its truth insight into the sources of its truth; the apogogical proof, on the other hand, while it can yield certainty, cannot enable us to comprehend truth in its connection with the grounds of its possibility.[91]

With these three rules as guides, Kant is ready to supply his first proof for transcendental idealism. He believes the conclusion that we are capable of experience is now well established. A necessary condition of experience, however, is the presence of synthetic a priori principles. Thus, synthetic a priori principles exist. There are three possible sources of such principles: they could be directly received from external nature (things-in-themselves), the world could be a transcendentally ideal mental construct, or they could be implanted innately by some spirit of truth. Eliminatively, Kant argues that because we cannot get a priori principles directly from nature and we have not been implanted with

---

[90] Ibid., A787/B815.
[91] Ibid., A789/B817.

synthetic knowledge by any divine spirit, the world must be transcendentally ideal.[92]

c. Conditions for the Possibility of Geometry

Kant writes, "Geometry is a science which determines the properties of space synthetically, and yet, *a priori*. What, then, must be our representation of space, in order that such knowledge of it may be possible?"[93] In this section, I hope to reconstruct Kant's argument for the possibility of geometry as a successful pure and applied science. This, we will see, will also constitute a second argument for transcendental idealism.

Geometry concerns space, including the empirically real space of physical objects; thus it must be synthetic. But geometry must be strictly universal and necessary; thus, a priori. Therefore, geometric principles are synthetic a priori judgments. But they can only be synthetic if they are intuitional, since (see section II-b) intuitions and concepts are the only modes of knowledge, and geometry could not arise from mere concepts. Further, they can only be a priori if the geometer's space is a priori and determines empirical space, where physical objects reside. And all of these conditions depend on the fact that space is simply the *form* of outer sense (see II-a and II-b). And finally, space can only be the form of outer sense if the objects of our experience are transcendentally ideal.[94]

---

[92] Ibid., B5; A93–94/B126; A216–217/B263–264.

[93] Ibid., B40–41.

[94] Ibid., A26–31/B42–45.

So transcendental idealism becomes a necessary condition for the possibility of geometry, and since it is well established that we can do geometry, Kant reasons, the doctrine of transcendental idealism must be correct. We may break the necessary conditions of geometry down if we like to show that Kant supplies the conditions for geometry both as a successful pure science and as an applied one. To be a successful pure science, space and the shapes and figures of geometry must be a priori intuitions. To be a successful applied science, the geometer's constructed space must determine the shared, empirically real space in which we live and make empirical observations. Since he establishes both of these conditions in his argument for the transcendental conditions for mathematics, he reasons that mathematics is possible both as a successful pure and a successful applied science, and it is guaranteed so by the very doctrine of transcendental idealism.

d. First Antinomy

An antinomy is a seemingly valid argument with a seemingly contradictory conclusion, or in this case, a set of seemingly valid arguments with seemingly contradictory conclusions. In his first antinomy, Kant advances an apparently sound thesis together with a seemingly contradictory but equally apparently sound antitheses. His thesis is that the "world has a beginning in time ... and is ... limited ... in space."[95] The antithesis of this thesis is that the "world has no beginning,

---

[95] Ibid., A426/454.

and no limits in space; it is infinite … [in] time and space."[96] Next, he shows both the thesis and the antithesis to be apparently sound by appealing to well-established proofs. But of course, as reason dictates, they cannot both be true.

Kant resolves this conflict by arguing that the antinomy rests on a false dichotomy. The thesis seems to be true because the world cannot be infinite; therefore it must be finite. The antithesis seems to be true because the world cannot be finite; thus, it must be infinite.[97] However, Kant maintains that finite and infinite are not contradictory opposites. Rather, they are contrary opposites, both of which can be false. He writes, "Thus the antinomy of pure reason in its cosmological ideas vanishes when it is shown that it is merely dialectical, and that it is a conflict due to an illusion which arises from our applying to appearances that exist only in our representations …"[98] This resolution to the problem of antinomies also gives us Kant's third argument for transcendental idealism, for it shows that if we hold to a notion of the world as a thing-in-itself existing in itself, we will have antinomies such as this one. Kant sums up this final argument succinctly, writing that the antinomy …

> affords indirect proof of the transcendental
> ideality of appearances—a proof which ought
> to convince any who may not be satisfied by
> the direct proof given in the Transcendental

---

[96] Ibid., A427/B455.

[97] Ibid., A428–429/B456–457.

[98] Ibid., A506/B534.

Aesthetic. This proof would consist in the following dilemma. If the world is a whole existing in itself, it is either finite or infinite. But both alternatives are false ... It is therefore also false that the world ... is a whole existing in itself. From this it then follows that appearances in general are nothing outside our representations—which is just what is meant by their transcendental ideality.[99]

---

[99] Ibid., A506–507/B534–535.

IV

SUMMARY OF PART 1

In section I of part 1 of this book, I explained what Kant means by a critique of pure reason and discussed his view of metaphysics and synthetic a priori judgments. The reader will recall Kant's assertion that metaphysical principles must be synthetic a priori judgments, and therefore, synthetic a priori judgments are a necessary though not sufficient condition for the success of metaphysics. The principles of natural science and mathematics were also said to be a priori and synthetic, so the success of these disciplines likewise presupposed the existence and justification of a priori synthetic judgments.

In section II, I explained Kant's notion of experience, along with many of its constituent parts, and showed how Kant was able to *save the appearances* by transforming them into experience. In section III, I discussed the doctrine of transcendental idealism and presented Kant's three arguments for this doctrine. The first, in the form of a transcendental proof, demonstrated that experience presupposes transcendental idealism. This proof is meant to put experience on a sure footing and thereby demonstrate the possibility of the success of natural science. The second proof, which argues that geometry presupposes transcendental idealism, can be seen as an argument restoring the possibility of mathematics (specifically, geometry). The final argument, the so-called first antinomy, shows that antinomies of reason can be avoided only by accepting transcendental idealism. Further, this argument addresses the possibility of metaphysics. However, Kant believes that since its principles lie beyond all possible experience, we cannot have synthetic a priori knowledge of metaphysics, and thus, transcendent philosophy remains transcendent. The crucial questions of metaphysics—for example, the existence of God—are, however, still legitimately accessible by faith.[100]

---

[100] Ibid., A745/B773.

PART 2

In part 2 of this book, I will discuss some of the central problems of Kant's *Critique of Pure Reason* and will show how he attempts to rescue immanent metaphysics, the metaphysics of nature upon which the foundations of other important sciences rest, from the dogmatic rationalism, idealism, and skepticism of the seventeenth and eighteenth centuries. In so doing, it will be necessary to reconstruct some critical arguments and recount some important distinctions. Among the topics that I will address are the categories of understanding, the forms of judgment, general logic, transcendental logic, and the logic of special employment, phoronomy, dynamics, mechanics, and phenomenology, and his table of principles (including the axioms of intuition, the anticipations of perception, the analogies of experience, and the postulates of empirical thought in general). Further, I will present his distinctions between regulative and constituitive uses of ideas, receptivity and spontaneity, and understanding and sensibility. Some of these topics will be discussed at length; others, only briefly. However, I wish to concentrate my attention on Kant's grand project, the way appearances are transformed into experience, the way material idealism, dogmatic rationalism, and empirical skepticism are refuted, and the way that he purports to save immanent metaphysics while rejecting transcendent metaphysics. To put this project in perspective, it is necessary to begin with a discussion of the scientific and philosophical setting in which Kant was working.

I

THE PROBLEM AND THE SETTING

Kant's critique was a thorough and critical self-examination of the scope and limits of human reason by reason. The motivation for this critique was largely to find out to what extent (if any) metaphysics was possible as a successful science. Without such a critique, of course, "either affirming or denying the possibility of metaphysics is sheer dogmatism."[101] It was of utmost importance to put (at least some of) metaphysics on a sure footing, because other important subjects rely on metaphysics for their principles. For example, Kant believed, natural science, ethics, and religion[102] could not be done without metaphysics. The problem with securing metaphysics is that its propositions lie beyond all possible experience yet must be necessary and universal. Thus, if metaphysical propositions exist at all,

---

[101] Werner S. Pluhar, translator's introduction to Immanuel Kant's *Critique of Judgment* (Indianapolis: Hackett, 1987), xxx.

[102] Ibid., xxxi.

they must be both synthetic and a priori. Thus, the crucial problem: How are synthetic a priori judgments justified?

Kant was impressed and inspired by Copernicus, who also held reason as the highest tribunal of knowledge. Kant writes, "Copernicus ... dared, in a manner contradictory of the senses, but yet true, to seek the observed movements, not in the heavenly bodies, but in the spectator."[103] Through his careful and rational approach to astronomy, Copernicus "changed the reference point of the solar system"[104] and in so doing was able to explain and predict the appearances of the heavens more perfectly than any previous thinker.[105]

But after Copernicus, philosophers and scientists became dogmatic about reason and the possibility of metaphysics. Kant was trained in the "rationalistic metaphysical tradition of ... Leibniz ... and his disciple Wolff ... [who] regarded the world as, in principle, knowable *a priori*."[106] This worldview, however, had two crucial flaws: it led inevitably to antinomies,[107] and it rested upon the "mediating intervention of a Deity[,]"[108] which Kant thought unsatisfactory. Descartes and Berkeley each tried to secure science and metaphysics through some type of material idealism. Kant writes, "Idealism—meaning thereby *material* idealism—is

---

[103] Immanuel Kant, *Critique of Pure Reason,* trans. Norman Kemp Smith (New York: St. Martin's, 1929, copyright 1781), Bxxiii n.

[104] Michael R. Matthews, *The Scientific Background to Modern Philosophy* (Indianapolis: Hackett, 1989), 35.

[105] Ibid., 33–34.

[106] Pluhar, xxxi.

[107] Ibid., xxxi.

[108] *Critique of Pure Reason,* B293.

the theory which declares the existence of objects in space outside us either to be merely doubtful and indemonstrable or to be false and impossible. The former is the *problematic* idealism of Descartes, which holds that there is only one empirical assertion that is indubitably certain, namely, that 'I am'. The latter is the *dogmatic* idealism of Berkeley."[109] Far from embracing this proposed solution, Kant shows his disdain for material idealism, writing, "it still remains a scandal to philosophy and to human reason in general that the existence of things outside us ... must be accepted merely on *faith* ..."[110]

Hume, Kant maintained, rightly rejected the rationalism of Leibniz and Wolff and the idealism of Berkeley and Descartes. However, Kant believed that Hume fell into an *equally dogmatic* skepticism.[111] One of the reasons Kant was unwilling to accept Humean skepticism was that Newton and other scientists had recently enjoyed much success, and of course, the success and empirical validity of science depended upon the existence of synthetic a priori metaphysical propositions. Werner Pluhar writes, "How are synthetic judgments possible a priori? *That* they were possible *a priori* was suggested strongly by Newton's success in natural science."[112] Kant was convinced that almost everything Newton had discovered and postulated was correct. Kant writes, "the true method of metaphysics is basically the same as that introduced by Newton into

---

[109] Ibid., B274.
[110] Ibid., Bxl n.
[111] Pluhar, xxxii.
[112] Ibid., xxxii.

natural science and which had such useful consequences in that field."[113] In fact, the methodology of Kant's first critique itself may have been motivated by Newton's maxim that "As in Mathematics, so in Natural Philosophy, the Investigation of difficult things by the Method of Analysis ought ever to precede the Method of Composition."[114] However impressed Kant was with Newton, he still believed Newton to be working under some unjustified assumptions, including material atomism.[115] So the metaphysical foundations of science still needed securing.

Later, I will show how Kant rescues immanent metaphysics from skepticism, material idealism, and dogmatic rationalism. In addition, I will show how his objective *transcendental idealism* replaces Descartes's existential *problematic idealism*. Presently, however, I must turn to a more detailed examination of some of the problems of the first critique.

---

[113] Matthews, 134; quoting Kant's *Selected Pre-Critical Writings and Correspondence with Beck*, trans. Kenford and Walton (Manchester: Manchester University Press, 1968), 17.

[114] Ibid., 134; quoting Newton's *Opticks* (New York: Dover, 1979), 404.

[115] James W. Ellington, translator's introduction to Immanuel Kant's *Metaphysical Foundations of Natural Science: Philosophy of Material Nature* (Indianapolis: Hackett, 1985).

II

THE CATEGORIES OF THE UNDERSTANDING

To have an objectively valid experience, as I will later show, requires understanding, sensibility, and the mediation of imagination. To comprehend what is meant by understanding, in Kant's sense, it is crucial that we understand the *categories*. Kant repeatedly refers to the categories as the *concepts of pure understanding*.[116] But what does this mean? The categories are often incompletely described as conceptual "glasses" or "lenses" through which we see the world, or as molds that give shape to our perceptions. But these descriptions fall short, partly because they neglect the *constructive* aspect of the categories. Pluhar articulates this forgotten aspect well when he writes that categories are "forms of thought that we have in our understanding and that we 'build', as it were, into the world."[117] Again: "Hence the categories *form* part of (enter into) all empirical concepts."[118] So categories are those "pure

---

[116] *Critique of Pure Reason,* A85/B118, A80–81/B106–7, A119.

[117] Pluhar, xxxiii.

[118] Ibid., xxxv; italics added for emphasis.

a priori modes of knowledge"[119] under which perceptions must be *subsumed* before we can have any meaningful empirical experience of the world, and that, in fact, help us construct that meaningful experience.[120] Without these concepts, we could not "*understand* anything in the manifold of intuition …"[121] It is important to understand that "the possibility of a thing cannot be determined from the category alone,"[122] nor can any "synthetic proposition be made from mere categories."[123] The categories are, however, necessary (although certainly not sufficient) for making synthetic a priori judgments and for establishing the metaphysical principles of our sciences.[124] Here, finally, is the complete table of all the categories of pure understanding:[125]

of Quantity	of Quality	of Relation	of Modality
unity	reality	of inherence and subsistence	possibility-impossibility
plurality	negation	of causality and dependence	existence-non-existence
totality	limitation	of community	necessity-contingency

[119] *Critique of Pure Reason*, A119.
[120] See *Prolegomena*, §22.
[121] *Critique of Pure Reason*, A80/B106.
[122] Ibid., A235/B288.
[123] Ibid., B289.
[124] See Pluhar, xxxiii.
[125] *Critique of Pure Reason*, A80/B106.

III

THE FORMS OF JUDGMENT

As I mentioned in section I-d of part 1, judgments, in general, are of terrific importance for Kant, because he holds that *all knowledge is discursive*.[126] Judgments are essentially the "mediate knowledge of an object"[127] and the "functions of unity among our representations[.]"[128] In the *Prolegomena,* he writes, "The uniting of representations in a consciousness is judgment. Thinking therefore is the same as judging ..."[129] All acts of understanding, then, are judgments, and the understanding itself can be called the *faculty of judgment*.[130] Just as there are only a finite number of pure concepts (in fact, twelve) from which we build our experience of the world, so too, when we examine our judging, we find that there are only the same number of *forms of judgment*.[131]

---

[126] Ibid., A68/B93.
[127] Ibid., A68/B93.
[128] Ibid., A69/B94.
[129] *Prolegomena,* §22.
[130] *Critique of Pure Reason,* A69/B94.
[131] Ibid., A70/B95.

That is, there are only twelve kinds of judgments that we can make.

These twelve forms of judgment are, in fact, necessarily[132] related to the categories of understanding. Kant writes, "There can be no question that in this enquiry [to find the judgments of understanding] our table of categories is the natural and safe guide. For since it is through the relation of the categories to possible experience that all pure *a priori* knowledge of understanding has to be constituted, their relation to sensibility in general will exhibit completely and systematically all the transcendental principles of the use of the understanding."[133] Here, again, is the complete list of the forms of judgment, which are related to the categories:[134]

Quantity	Quality	Relation	Modality
universal	affirmative	categorical	problematic
particular	negative	hypothetical	assertoric
singular	infinite	disjunctive	apodeictic

---

[132] By *necessity,* I do not here mean logical necessity but rather law-like or nomological necessity, as Kant sometimes uses the term.

[133] *Critique of Pure Reason,* A148/B187–188.

[134] Ibid., A70/B95.

IV

THE PRINCIPLES OF PURE UNDERSTANDING

The twelve categories, Kant says, lead us to discover the a priori synthetic principles of the understanding. The same categories also naturally guide us "in the construction of the table of principles. For the latter are simply *rules for the objective employment of the former.*"[135] As with the categories and the principles of understanding, there are four sets of principles, or rules for applying the categories. These are as follows: (1) the axioms of intuition, (2) the anticipations of perception, (3) the analogies of experience, and (4) the postulates of empirical thought in general.[136] In addition, each of these sets of principles corresponds to a particular field of science. Each of these fields poses a different *definition of matter.* Although I cannot present a detailed discussion of each rule and each science in this brief guide, I will recount in summary (relying heavily on Kant's

---

[135] Ibid., A161/B200; italics added.
[136] Ibid., A161/B200.

own words) each set and the scientific field to which each principle corresponds.

The *axioms of intuition* inform us that "All intuitions are extensive magnitudes."[137] In other words, all intuitional objects are capable of being measured and so are subject to the normal laws of mathematics and geometry. The scientific field that corresponds to the axioms of intuition is *phoronomy,* the physics of motion. In his *Metaphysical Foundations of Natural Science*, Kant explicates the laws of phoronomy in several ways. The most essential explication of phoronomy says that "Matter is the movable in space. That space which is itself movable is called material, or also relative, space; that in which all motion must ultimately be thought (which is itself therefore absolutely immovable) is called pure, or absolute space."[138] He shows that any motion can be viewed as moving in relation to immovable space, or as space moving in relation to an object at rest.

In regard to the principle of the *anticipations of perception,* Kant writes, "In all appearances, the real that is an object of sensation has intensive magnitude, that is, a degree."[139] In other words, it has an intensity, or "a degree of influence on the sense ..."[140] The anticipations of perception relate to the field of *dynamics.* Kant provides six definitions and eight propositions, or theorems, of dynamics. The gist of

---

[137] Ibid., B202.

[138] Kant, *Metaphysical Foundations of Natural Science: Philosophy of Material Nature* (Indianapolis: Hackett, 1985), AK 480.

[139] *Critique of Pure Reason,* B207.

[140] Ibid., B202.

dynamics is that matter must be governed by the discovered laws of attractive and repulsive force.[141]

There are three *analogies of experience*, which together assert that "Experience is possible only through the representation of a necessary connection of perceptions."[142] Kant's first analogy, the principle of permanence of substance, claims that substance does not come into being or pass away: "In all change of appearance substance is permanent ..."[143] The second analogy, the principle of succession in time, in accordance with the law of causality, can be viewed as Kant's answer to Hume's skepticism concerning causality. Kant writes, "All alterations take place in conformity with the law of the connection of cause and effect."[144] Further, he argues that we must "derive the *subjective succession* of apprehension from the *objective succession* of appearances. Otherwise the order of apprehension is entirely undetermined, and does not distinguish one appearance from another."[145] We determine this objective succession in accordance with the rules of force. This prioritizing of the objective over the subjective is a theme in Kant's philosophy and will make up part of his refutation of Descartes's *problematic idealism,* as I will soon show. The third analogy, the principle of coexistence, says "All substances, in so far as they can be perceived to coexist in space, are in thoroughgoing reciprocity."[146] The

---

[141] *Metaphysical Foundations,* AK 496–535.

[142] *Critique of Pure Reason,* B218.

[143] Ibid., A182; see also B232.

[144] Ibid., B232.

[145] Ibid., A193/B238.

[146] Ibid., A211/B256.

three analogies correspond to three laws of *mechanics.* These are in brief that the quantity of matter is unchanging, that any change in matter is caused by an external force, and for every action, there is an equal reaction.[147]

The *postulates of empirical thought* seem to contain two distinct but related parts: the definitions of the important terms, *possible, actual,* and *necessary,* and a refutation of material idealism. The definitions are as follows:

1. That which agrees with the formal conditions of experience, that is, with the conditions of intuition and of concepts, is *possible.*

2. That which is bound up with the material conditions of experience, that is, with sensations, is *actual.*

3. That which in its connection with the actual is determined in accordance with universal conditions of experience is … *necessary.*[148]

Kant undercuts material idealism (of Descartes and Berkeley) by arguing that "The mere, but empirically determined, consciousness of my own existence proves the

[147] *Metaphysical Foundations,* AK 536–553.
[148] *Critique of Pure Reason,* A218/B265–266.

existence of objects in space outside me."[149] He argues this, writing:

> I am conscious of my own existence as determined in time. All determination of time presupposes something *permanent* in perception. This permanent cannot, however, be something in me, since it is only through this permanent that my existence in time can itself be determined. Thus perception of this permanent is possible only through a *thing* outside me and not through the mere *representation* of a thing outside me; and consequently the determination of my existence in time is possible only through the existence of actual things which I perceive outside me.[150]

The material idealism of Berkeley and Descartes assumed that only inner experience was immediately knowable, and from our inner experience, we infer the existence of things outside of us. Like Copernicus, who changed the reference point of the universe, Kant changes the reference point of knowledge by showing that outer experience is really immediate, and only by means of it do we have consciousness of our own existence in time.[151] With this revolutionary move, Kant replaces the *subjective* Cartesian existential

---

[149] Ibid., B275.
[150] Ibid., B275.
[151] Ibid., B276–277.

epistemology with a new *objective* epistemology, which holds the empirical experience of the external world as a condition of our own subjective perceptions and observations. (One is reminded of Heidegger's criticism of Sartre's existentialism, when Heidegger claimed that Sartre's philosophy was purely subjective and thus said nothing about the real world. Heidegger, here, was perhaps inspired by Kant's refutation of idealism.)

The postulates of empirical thought directly correspond to the field of *phenomenology,* the science of transforming appearances into objectively valid experience through the determination of empirically valid motions. Phenomenology, according to Kant, says that the motion of matter is necessarily relative to some matter outside itself, and consequently, this other matter's motion is relative to the former matter.[152]

Before I leave the principles of pure understanding behind for a discussion of Kant's logic, I must make one final distinction, which will be of importance in section VI. The four sets of principles discussed in this section can be divided into the *mathematical* and the *dynamic principles.* The mathematical principles, which contain the axioms of intuition and the anticipations of perception, are those ideas that govern the use of the categories of quality and quantity. The dynamic principles, on the other hand, the analogies of experience and the postulates of empirical thought in general, control the use of the categories of relation and modality.

---

[152] *Metaphysical Foundations,* AK 554–565.

V

LOGIC

Another vital part of the understanding is *logic*, which Kant defines as "the rules of the understanding in general ..."[153] Although some types of logic are *applied* to specific empirical propositions, logic itself is concerned only with the *form* of reasoning, not the *matter*. Kant writes, logic "has no touchstone for the discovery of such error as concerns not the form but the content."[154] Logic can be split into three basic types: the logic of special employment, general logic, and transcendental logic. Kant initially distinguishes only between the first two: "Logic ... can be treated in a twofold manner, either as logic of the general or as logic of the special employment of the understanding."[155] Of these two, the logic of special employment seems to be the least complicated and, given the brevity with which Kant speaks of it, the least important. This sort of logic is the specific set of rules (logical requirements) that pertain to a particular

---

[153] *Critique of Pure Reason,* A52/B76.

[154] Ibid., A60/B84.

[155] Ibid., A52/B76.

discipline or field. General logic, on the other hand, is not concerned with any specific science. It abstracts from all content.[156]

General logic can be broken down into two further types—pure and applied general logic. Kant writes:

> General logic is either pure or applied. In the former we abstract from all empirical conditions under which our understanding is exercised, *i.e.* from the influence of the senses, the play of imagination, the laws of memory, the force of habit, inclination, etc., and so from all sources of prejudice, indeed from all causes from which this or that knowledge may arise or seem to arise.[157]

He continues, "Pure general logic has to do, therefore, only with principles *a priori,* and is a *canon of understanding* and of reason, but only in respect of what is formal in their employment."[158] Again: pure general logic "has nothing to do with empirical principles …"[159] Applied general logic *is* concerned with certain empirical propositions: "General logic is called applied, when it is directed to the rules of the employment of understanding under the subjective empirical conditions dealt with by psychology."[160]

---

[156] Ibid., A55/B79.
[157] Ibid., A52–53/B77.
[158] Ibid., A53/B77.
[159] Ibid., A54/B78.
[160] Ibid., A53/B77.

Kant describes general logic as a *mere canon of judgment*.[161] While it can be employed as a tool to bring a multitude of representations under one concept, it cannot be used as an *organon*, or instrument, to further the content of knowledge. If it is so employed, it will be "a logic of illusion, that is *dialectical*."[162] (Dialectic, for Kant, has two meanings. First, it is the *illusion* that general logic can be used in supporting positive claims about the content of knowledge.[163] Second, it is the *critique of this illusion*.[164] Kant is, here, using dialectic in the former sense.) "For," he continues, "logic teaches us nothing whatsoever regarding the content of knowledge, but lays down only the formal conditions of agreement with the understanding."[165] "The explanation of the possibility of synthetic judgments is a problem with which general logic has nothing to do."[166] Transcendental logic, however, is concerned with such judgments. Kant writes, "transcendental logic is in position completely to fulfil its ultimate purpose, that of determining the scope and limits of pure understanding."[167] In a fuller passage, Kant differentiates transcendental logic from general logic, saying:

---

[161] Ibid., A61/B85.

[162] Ibid., A61/B86.

[163] Ibid., A61/B86.

[164] Ibid., A62/B86–87.

[165] Ibid., A61/B86.

[166] Ibid., A154/B193.

[167] Ibid., A154/B193.

> General logic, as has been repeatedly said, abstracts from all content of knowledge, and looks to some other source, whatever that may be, for the representations which it is to transform into concepts by process of analysis. Transcendental logic, on the other hand, has lying before it a manifold of *a priori* sensibility.[168]

Again: "By means of analysis different representations are brought under one concept—a procedure treated of in general logic. What transcendental logic, on the other hand, teaches, is how we bring to concepts, not representations, but the *pure synthesis* of representations."[169] Finally:

> Such a science, which should determine the origin, the scope, and the objective validity of such knowledge, would have to be called *transcendental logic,* because unlike general logic ... [it] concerns itself with the laws of understanding and the reason solely in so far as they relate *a priori* to objects.[170]

In other words, transcendental logic is the logic of a priori synthetic judgments, and it is through transcendental logic

---

[168] Ibid., A76/B102.
[169] Ibid., A78/B104.
[170] Ibid., AA57/B81–82.

(only) that we can come to see the justification of the a priori synthetic propositions of immanent metaphysics.

Like general logic, transcendental logic can be split into two distinct types. These are *transcendental analytic logic* and *transcendental dialectic logic*. Kant writes, "The part of transcendental logic which deals with the elements of the pure knowledge yielded by the understanding, and the principles without which no object can be thought, is transcendental analytic. It is a logic of truth."[171] This logic, Kant continues, "should only be used as a canon for passing judgment upon the empirical employment of the understanding, it is misapplied if appealed to as an organon of its general and unlimited application."[172] The transcendental dialectic logic, on the other hand, "must form a critique of this dialectical illusion"[173] of the misapplied analytic logic and "expose the false, illusory character of [their] groundless pretensions …"[174]

Thus, in addition to logic being an essential part of the understanding, namely its a priori rules, it also serves a significant purpose to Kant's grand project: transcendental analytic logic serves to justify synthetic a priori judgments, and transcendental dialectical logic acts as a negative touchstone, to keep reason in check, to keep it from being used dogmatically in attempt to extend the content of knowledge beyond all possible experience. This is, essentially, we will see, the way Kant rescues immanent metaphysics while

---

[171] Ibid., A63/B87.

[172] Ibid., A63/B88.

[173] Ibid., A63/B88.

[174] Ibid., A63–64/B88.

rejecting transcendent metaphysics. While propositions of immanent metaphysics are capable of being supported by transcendental analytic logic, transcendental metaphysics relies upon logic as an organon of truth, as opposed to merely a canon. Therefore, transcendental metaphysics is dogmatic, or what Kant calls dialectical (in the former sense).

VI

REGULATIVE AND CONSTITUITIVE IDEAS

Before graduating on to the big picture of Kant's philosophy, there is one more issue I must briefly address. This is the important distinction that Kant makes between *regulative* and *constituitive* uses of ideas. The use of an idea is constitiutive if it is "of such a character that … we can regard it as proving the truth of the universal rule which we have adopted as hypothesis."[175] If it governs but cannot prove the truth of a rule, it is merely regulative. These uses can be constituitive or merely regulative as regards either intuition or experience. Principles that are constituitive of intuition allow us to produce intuitions from sensations.[176] Included among those ideas that are constituitive of intuition are the mathematical principles (the axioms of intuition and the anticipations of perception) discussed in section IV of this part. The dynamic principles (the analogies of experience and the postulates of empirical thought in general), on the

---

[175] Ibid., A647/B675.
[176] Ibid., A179/B220.

other hand, are merely regulative of intuition. However, they are constituitive of experience. In other words, they cannot produce intuitions from sensations, but they can, and in fact do, enable us to order our intuitions in such a way as to aid our objectively valid experience of the world. Finally, maxims of reason (our transcendental ideas) are merely regulative of experience.

Kant claims that "When merely regulative principles are treated as constituitive, and are therefore employed as objective principles, they may come into conflict with one another."[177] This is the mistake that the dogmatic rationalists, who assumed transcendent metaphysics to be possible, made, and the conflict Kant is speaking of can be seen in the antinomies of pure reason. He writes, "I accordingly maintain that transcendental ideas never allow of any constituitive employment. When regarded in that mistaken manner, and therefore, as supplying concepts of certain objects, they are but pseudo-rational, merely dialectical concepts."[178]

---

[177] Ibid., A647/B675.
[178] Ibid., A644/B672; see also A666/B694, A669/B697, A680/B708, and *Prolegomena*, §56.

VII

Experience (Revisited)

Part of the big picture of Kant's philosophy is his account of how experience and the knowledge of that experience is possible. All knowledge, Kant claims, springs from two interconnected sources of the mind: *receptivity* and *spontaneity*.[179] Receptivity is the mind's "power of receiving representations."[180] Spontaneity is the "power of knowing an object through these representations."[181] "Through the first," writes Kant, "an object is *given* to us, through the second the object is *thought* in relation to that [given] representation ..."[182] The former is the faculty of intuitions; the latter, of concepts. Thus, Kant concludes, "Intuitions and concepts constitute ... the elements of our knowledge, so that neither concepts without an intuition in some way corresponding to them, nor intuition without concepts, can yield knowledge."[183]

---

[179] Ibid., A50/B74.

[180] Ibid., A51/B75.

[181] Ibid., A50/B74.

[182] Ibid., A50/B74.

[183] Ibid., A50/B74.

Intuitions, the reader may remember,[184] are a product of the sensibility, while concepts are a product of the understanding.[185] Thus, sensibility and understanding must unite to form knowledge. However, this union requires a mediation in the form of the faculty of imagination. Kant writes:

> The two extremes, namely sensibility and understanding, must stand in necessary condition with each other through the mediation of this transcendental function of imagination, because otherwise the former, though indeed yielding appearances, would supply no objects of empirical knowledge, and consequently, no experience.[186]

Again: This "[s]ynthesis … is the mere result of the power of imagination."[187] Or finally: "Experience … rests on the synthetic unity of appearances, that is, on a synthesis according to concepts of an object of appearances in general. Apart from such synthesis it would not be knowledge."[188] So experience and, likewise, knowledge of that experience is a synthetic union of all the aspects of the understanding and of the sensibility, under the mediation of imagination. In this way only is objectively valid experience possible.

---

[184] From part 1.

[185] See *Critique of Pure Reason,* A67–68/B92; *Prologomena,* §21a–22, §36.

[186] *Critique of Pure Reason,* A124.

[187] Ibid., A78/B103.

[188] Ibid., A156/B195.

VIII

METAPHYSICS

Another central theme of Kant's first critique is how he purports to save immanent metaphysics while rejecting transcendent metaphysics. By *immanent metaphysics,* Kant means the "metaphysics of nature. Such a metaphysics cannot tell us anything about the supersensible."[189] In his critique of the scope and nature of reason, he finds that general logic is often incorrectly used by thinkers. Specifically, it is used to extend the content of knowledge. But general logic has no governance over the matter of knowledge, only the form. Thus, any beliefs that it produces will be merely dialectical. Similarly, although transcendental analytic logic is capable of helping to justify synthetic a priori judgments, it must be kept in check by the transcendental dialectic. Otherwise, it may extend beyond all possible experience. This, too, would be dialectical. Further, merely regulative ideas are often used as constituitive (and hence, dialectical), in an attempt to prove something with which it has nothing to do. This attempt leads to conflicts, namely the antinomies

---

[189] Pluhar, xxxix.

of pure reason. So, Kant concludes, only those *laws* that are necessary but still within the domain of possible experience are knowable.[190]

"[Hence]," as Pluhar writes, "we can have a 'metaphysics' in the sense of the *a priori* principles of all possible objects of experience."[191] Anything beyond, however, would be dialectical. Kant writes, "all those conclusions of ours which profess to lead us beyond the field of possible experience are deceptive and without foundation."[192] Pluhar summarizes Kant's position on the possibility of metaphysics well, writing:

> Thus the *Critique of Pure Reason* pays the price of renouncing claims to theoretical knowledge where it was sought most eagerly, but it does at least rescue immanent metaphysics, and with it natural science, from dogmatic rationalism with its unjustifiable and contradictory claims, and from the skepticism of dogmatic empiricism.[193]

---

[190] Ibid., xxxii.
[191] Ibid., xxxiii.
[192] *Critique of Pure Reason*, A642/B670.
[193] Pluhar, xxxix.

IX

REFUTATION OF SKEPTICISM, IDEALISM, AND DOGMATIC RATIONALISM

In this final section, I would like to summarize the arguments that Kant poses against three influential philosophies of the seventeenth and eighteenth centuries: empirical skepticism, dogmatic rationalism, and material idealism.

It seems that Kant makes (at least) five separate attacks on the empirical skepticism of Hume, although not all of these are explicit: (1) Kant accuses the skeptic of being dogmatic because he has not undergone a thorough critique of his method. (2) The success of Newton in natural science supports the existence of objectively valid, necessary, and universal laws of natural science. (3) Hume's skepticism about causality is proven incorrect, as Kant shows that all changes occur in accordance with the law of cause and effect, and this relationship is determined objectively through the rules of force. (4) Kant demonstrates how immanent metaphysics is possible and thus secures the principles of natural science. And (5) Kant demonstrates how *experience* is possible in an objective and empirically valid way.

There seem to be three attacks made on the rationalism of Leibniz and Wolff: (1) As with Humean skepticism, no critique of method has been made, and thus, it is merely dogmatic. (2) The rationalists operate under the unjustified and, in fact, incorrect assumption that merely regulative or merely logical propositions can be used to extend the content of knowledge. The inevitable consequence of this is, of course, antinomies. (3) Rationalism must rely on the mediating influence of a deity, of whom we can have no possible experience. Kant writes, "the wildest hypotheses, if only they are physical, are here more tolerable than a hyperphysical hypothesis, such as an appeal to a divine Author, assumed simply in order that we may have an explanation."[194]

Kant, likewise, seems to have (at least) three arguments against material idealism: (1) The mere notion that we must accept the existence of the outside world on faith is inconsistent with (is, indeed, an affront to) reason. (2) While the idealists derive the existence of the external world (if they do at all) from inner sense, Kant shows that personal existence is actually dependent upon the existence of something outside us. In the preface to the second edition of the first critique, Kant writes, "But through inner *experience* I am conscious of *my existence* in time ... and this is more than to be conscious merely of my representation. It is identical with the *empirical consciousness of my existence,* which is determinable only through relation to something

---

[194] *Critique of Pure Reason,* A773/B801.

which … is outside me."[195] (3) Kant further shows that the knowledge of the succession of events in time is likewise objective, not subjective. Thus, Kant creates a Copernican revolution in philosophy, turning epistemology away from subjective idealism and toward an objective and empirically valid transcendental idealism.

---

[195] Ibid., Bxi n.

CONCLUSION

Kant's first critique is not only one of the most important works in the history of Western philosophy; it is also one of the most fecund. Kant's *Critique of Pure Reason* directly motivated both the ascetic atheism of Schopenhauer and the German idealist philosophies of Hegel, Schelling, and Ficte, among others. In the twentieth and twenty-first centuries, the metaphysics and epistemology of Kant's first critique were of central concern to thinkers such as Quine, Grice and Strawson, Korsgaard, and Allen Wood.

In this brief guide, I have attempted to explicate several of the central arguments of Kant's *Critique of Pure Reason*, including his transcendental proof, transcendental idealism, and his refutation of skepticism, idealism, and dogmatic rationalism. Additionally, I have tried to make plain such Kantian ideas as synthetic, analytic, a priori, a posteriori, and regulative and constitutive judgments, experience, sensations, intuitions, and concepts, and the way in which the manifold of appearances can be transformed into objectively valid experience. I have discussed Kant's first antinomy and his conditions for the possibility of geometry as well as his categories of pure understanding, forms of judgment, and principles of pure reason, logic, and metaphysics. And I have attempted to present all of this against the historical backdrop of eighteenth-century science and philosophy.

I hope this short guide will serve as a helpful tutorial to Kant's masterwork. But of course, no single volume could elucidate the immense and intricate clockwork of the *Critique of Pure Reason*. For this reason, I have included some personal recommendations for further reading on Kant's first critique.

RECOMMENDATIONS FOR FURTHER READING

Adair-Toteff, C. "Immanuel Kant, Critique of Pure Reason." *British Journal for the History of Philosophy* 6 (1998): 297–298.

Allais, Lucy. "Kant, Non-Conceptual Content and the Representation of Space." *Journal of the History of Philosophy* 47, no. 3 (2009): 383–413.

Allison, Henry E. "The Non-Spatiality of Things in Themselves for Kant." *Journal of the History of Philosophy* 14, no. 3 (1976): 313–321.

Ameriks, Karl. *Interpreting Kant's Critiques.* Oxford University Press, 2003.

Baiasu, Sorin. "Space, Time and Mind-Dependence." *Kantian Review* 16, no. 2 (2011): 175–190.

Bernecker, Sven. "Kant on Spatial Orientation." *European Journal of Philosophy* 20, no. 4 (2012): 519–533.

Bouton, Christophe. "Transcendental Ideality or Absolute Reality of Time? Time for the Subject and Time for the World in Kant." *Kant-Studien* 103, no. 4 (2012).

Buroker, Jill Vance. *Kant's Critique of Pure Reason: An Introduction.* Cambridge University Press, 2006.

Callanan, John J. "Contemporary Kantian Metaphysics: New Essays on Space and Time." *International Journal of Philosophical Studies* 22, no. 1 (2014): 144–148.

Carrier, Martin. "Kant's Relational Theory of Absolute Space." *Kant-Studien* 83, no. 4 (1992): 399–416.

Cassirer, H. W. *Kant's First Critique: An Appraisal of the Permanent Significance of Kant's Critique of Pure Reason.* Routledge, 2002.

Chadwick, Ruth F., and Clive Cazeaux, eds. *Kant's Critique of Pure Reason.* Routledge, 1992.

Chignell, Andrew. "Kant's Concepts of Justification." *Noûs* 41, no. 1 (2007): 33–63.

Collins, Arthur W. *Possible Experience: Understanding Kant's Critique of Pure Reason.* University of California Press, 1999.

Constantin, Antonopoulos. "Passive Knowledge: How to Make Sense of Kant's A Priori—Or How Not to Be 'Too Busily Subsuming.'" *Open Journal of Philosophy* 1, no. 2 (2011): 39.

Dryer, D. P. "The Aim of the Critique of Pure Reason." *Dialogue* 2, no. 3 (1963): 301–312.

Edgar, Scott. "The Explanatory Structure of the Transcendental Deduction and a Cognitive Interpretation of the First Critique." *Canadian Journal of Philosophy* 40, no. 2 (2010): 285–314.

Ewing, A. C. *A Short Commentary on Kant's Critique of Pure Reason.* University of Chicago Press, 1987.

Ewing, A. C. "The Message of Kant." *Philosophy* 6, no. 21 (1931): 43–55.

Gardner, Sebastian. *Routledge Philosophy Guidebook to Kant and the Critique of Pure Reason.* Routledge, 1999.

Gardner, Sebastian, and Arthur Collins. "Kant and the Critique of Pure Reason." *Philosophical Quarterly* 50, no. 200 (2000): 391–395.

Gregor, Mary J. "Critique of Pure Reason." *Review of Metaphysics* 38, no. 1 (1984): 124–126.

Grier, M. "Possible Experience: Understanding Kant's Critique of Pure Reason." *Philosophical Review* 110, no. 1 (2001): 135–137.

Groth, Miles. "Phenomenological Interpretation of Kant's Critique of Pure Reason, Studies in Continental Thought." *Review of Metaphysics* 52, no. 2 (1998): 455–457.

Guyer, Paul, ed. *The Cambridge Companion to Kant's Critique of Pure Reason.* Cambridge University Press, 2010.

Guyer, Paul. *Kant.* Routledge, 2006.

Hacyan, Shahen. "On the Transcendental Ideality of Space and Time in Modern Physics." *Kant-Studien* 97, no. 3 (2006): 382–395.

Hall, Bryan, Mark Black, and Matt Sheffield. *The Arguments of Kant's Critique of Pure Reason.* Lexington Books, 2010.

Hartnack, Justus. *Kant's Theory of Knowledge: An Introduction to the Critique of Pure Reason.* Hackett, 2001.

Heidegger, Martin. *Phenomenological Interpretation of Kant's Critique of Pure Reason.* Indiana University Press, 1997.

Heidemann, Dietmar H., ed. *Kant and Non-Conceptual Content.* Routledge, 2012.

Hyslop, James H. "Kant's Doctrine of Time and Space." *Mind* 7, no. 25 (1898): 71–84.

Kitcher, Patricia, ed. *Kant's Critique of Pure Reason: Critical Essays.* Rowman & Littlefield Publishers, 1998.

Kuehn, Manfred. *Kant: A Biography.* Cambridge University Press, 2014.

Kuehn, Manfred. "Kant's Conception of 'Hume's Problem.'" *Journal of the History of Philosophy* 21, no. 2 (1983): 175–193.

Kuehn, Manfred. "Kant's Transcendental Deduction of God's Existence as a Postulate of Pure Practical Reason." *Kant-Studien* 76, nos. 1–4 (1985): 152–169.

Luchte, James. *Kant's Critique of Pure Reason: A Reader's Guide.* Continuum, 2007.

McBay Merritt, Melissa. "Analysis in the Critique of Pure Reason." *Kantian Review* 12, no. 1 (2007): 61–89.

McBay Merritt, Melissa. "Kant on the Transcendental Deduction of Space and Time: An Essay on the Philosophical Resources of the Transcendental Aesthetic." *Kantian Review* 14, no. 2 (2010): 1–37.

McBay Merritt, Melissa. "Science and the Synthetic Method of the Critique of Pure Reason." *Review of Metaphysics* 59, no. 3 (2006): 517–539.

McGoldrick, P. M. "The Metaphysical Exposition: An Analysis of the Concept of Space." *Kant-Studien* 76, nos. 1–4 (1985): 257–275.

McLear, Colin. "Two Kinds of Unity in the Critique of Pure Reason." *Journal of the History of Philosophy* 53, no. 1 (2015): 79–110.

Mead, Edwin D. "Kant's 'Critique of Pure Reason.'" *Journal of Speculative Philosophy* 15, no. 1 (1881): 95–98.

Melnick, Arthur. *Kant's Analogies of Experience.* University of Chicago Press, 1973.

Melnick, Arthur. "Kant on Intuition." *Midwest Studies in Philosophy* 8, no. 1 (1983): 339–358.

Melnick, Arthur. "Space, Time, and Thought in Kant." *Noûs* 28, no. 2 (1994): 258–262.

Miles, Murray. "Kant's 'Copernican Revolution': Toward Rehabilitation of a Concept and Provision of a Framework for the Interpretation of the Critique of Pure Reason." *Kant-Studien* 97, no. 1 (2006): 1–32.

Morris, George S. "Kant's Transcendental Deduction of Categories." *Journal of Speculative Philosophy* 15, no. 3 (1881): 253–274.

Newman, Michael D. "The Unity of Time and Space, and Its Role In Kant's Doctrine of Apriori Synthesis." *Idealistic Studies* 11, no. 2 (1981): 109–124.

O'Shea, James R. *Kant's Critique of Pure Reason: An Introduction and Interpretation.* Acumen, 2012.

Palter, Robert. "Absolute Space and Absolute Motion in Kant's Critical Philosophy." *Synthese* 23, no. 1 (1971): 47–62.

Paton, H. J. "Kant's First Critique." *Philosophical Quarterly* 6, no. 24 (1956): 260–265.

Paton, H. J. *Kant's Metaphysic of Experience.* G. Allen & Unwin, Ltd., 1936.

Reuscher, John A. *A Concordance to the Critique of Pure Reason.* P. Lang, 1996.

Ritchie, A. D. "Note on the Development of Kant's Thought in the Critique of Pure Reason." *Mind* 50, no. 198 (1941): 207–208.

Rogerson, Kenneth. "Kant on the Ideality of Space." *Canadian Journal of Philosophy* 18 (June 1988): 271–286.

Rosenberg, Jay F. *Accessing Kant: A Relaxed Introduction to the Critique of Pure Reason.* Oxford University Press, 2005.

Sassen, Brigitte, ed. *Kant's Early Critics: The Empiricist Critique of the Theoretical Philosophy.* Cambridge University Press, 2000.

Schipper, E. W. "Kant's Answer to Hume's Problem." *Kant-Studien* 53, nos. 1–4 (1962): 68–74.

Schönfeld, Martin. *The Philosophy of the Young Kant: The Precritical Project.* Oxford University Press, 2000.

Schurman, J. G. "Kant's Critical Problem: What is It in Itself and for Us?" *Philosophical Review* 2, no. 2 (1893): 129–166.

Scruton, Roger. *Kant: A Very Short Introduction.* Oxford University Press, 2001.

Shaw, Gisela. "Reason and Transcendence. An Introduction to Kant's Critique of Pure Reason." *Philosophy and History* 6, no. 2 (1973): 138–139.

Smit, Houston. "The Role of Reflection in Kant's Critique of Pure Reason." *Pacific Philosophical Quarterly* 80, no. 2 (1999): 203–223.

Smith, Norman Kemp. *A Commentary to Kant's 'Critique of Pure Reason.'* Palgrave Macmillan, 2003.

Smith, Norman Kemp. "Kant's Method of Composing the Critique of Pure Reason." *Philosophical Review* 24, no. 5 (1915): 526–532.

Srzednicki, Jan T. J. *The Place of Space and Other Themes: Variations on Kant's First Critique.* Kluwer, 1983.

Stang, Nicholas. "Kant on Complete Determination and Infinite Judgement." *British Journal for the History of Philosophy* 20, no. 6 (2012): 1117–1139.

Stapleford, Scott. "A Refutation of Idealism From 1777." *Idealistic Studies* 40, no. 1/2 (2010): 139–146.

Steinhoff, Gordon. "Strawson and the Refutation of Idealism." *Idealistic Studies* 20, no. 1 (1990): 61–81.

Stern, Robert. "Metaphysical Dogmatism, Humean Scepticism, Kantian Criticism." *Kantian Review* 11, no. 1 (2006): 102–116.

Stine, William D. "Self-Consciousness in Kant's 'Critique of Pure Reason.'" *Philosophical Studies* 28, no. 3 (1975): 189–197.

Stirling, J. Hutchison. "Kant has Not Answered Hume." *Mind* 10, no. 37 (1885): 45–72.

Strathern, Paul. *Kant in 90 Minutes.* Ivan R. Dee Publisher, 1996.

Strawson, P. F. *The Bounds of Sense: An Essay on Kant's Critique of Pure Reason.* Harper & Row, 1975.

Sullivan, Malachy R. "Kant's Critique of Pure Reason." *New Scholasticism* 34, no. 4 (1960): 531–533.

Tolley, Clinton. "The Generality of Kant's Transcendental Logic." *Journal of the History of Philosophy* 50, no. 3 (2012): 417–446.

Van Cleve, James. *Problems From Kant.* Oxford University Press, 1999.

van de Pitte, Frederick P. "A Companion to Kant's Critique of Pure Reason." *International Studies in Philosophy* 20, no. 1 (1988): 61.

Velkley, Richard. "Essays on Kant's Critique of Pure Reason." *Review of Metaphysics* 37, no. 4 (1984): 865–868.

Walsh, W. H. "Kant on the Perception of Time." *The Monist* 51, no. 3 (1967): 376–396.

Ward, Andrew. "Kant's First Analogy of Experience." *Kant-Studien* 92, no. 4 (2001): 387–406.

Warren, Daniel. "Kant and the Apriority of Space." *Philosophical Review* 107, no. 2 (1998): 179–224.

Watkins, Eric. "Critique of Pure Reason." *International Philosophical Quarterly* 39, no. 2 (1999): 235–237.

Watkins, Eric, ed. *Kant's Critique of Pure Reason: Background Source Materials.* Cambridge University Press, 2009.

Watkins, Eric. "Kant's Model of Causality: Causal Powers, Laws, and Kant's Reply to Hume." *Journal of the History of Philosophy* 42, no. 4 (2004): 449–488.

Waxman, Wayne. *Kant's Model of the Mind: A New Interpretation of Transcendental Idealism.* Oxford University Press, 1991.

Weier, Winfried. "A Metacritique of Kant's Critique of Reason." *International Philosophical Quarterly* 8, no. 3 (1968): 317–333.

Weldon, T. D. *Kant's Critique of Pure Reason.* Oxford, Clarendon Press, 1958.

Werkmeister, W. H. "The Critique of Pure Reason and Physics." *Kant-Studien* 68, nos. 1–4 (1977): 33–45.

Westphal, Kenneth R. "Affinity, Idealism and Naturalism: The Stability of Cinnabar and the Possibility of Experience." *Kant-Studien* 88, no. 2 (1997): 139–189.

Westphal, Kenneth R. "How Does Kant Prove That We Perceive, and Not Merely Imagine, Physical Objects?" *Review of Metaphysics* 59, no. 4 (2006): 781–806.

Westphal, Kenneth R. "Kant's Cognitive Semantics, Newton's Rule Four of Philosophy and Scientific Realism." *Bulletin of the Hegel Society of Great Britain* 63 (2011): 27–49.

Wilkerson, T. E. *Kant's Critique of Pure Reason: A Commentary for Students.* Clarendon Press, 1976.

Wilson, Eric Entrican. "On the Nature of Judgment in Kant's Transcendental Logic." *Idealistic Studies* 40, no. 1/2 (2010): 43–63.

Woelert, Peter. "Kant's Hands, Spatial Orientation, and the Copernican Turn." *Continental Philosophy Review* 40, no. 2 (2007): 139–150.

Wood, Allen W. *Kant.* Wiley-Blackwell, 2008.

Wood, Allen W. "Kant's Dialectic." *Canadian Journal of Philosophy* 5 (December 1975): 595–614.

Wood, Allen W. *Kant's Rational Theology.* Cornell University Press, 1978.

Wood, Allen W. "What is transcendental idealism?" *Endoxa* 18 (2004): 27–44.

Wood, Allen W., Paul Guyer & Henry E. Allison. "Debating Allison on Transcendental Idealism." *Kantian Review* 12, no. 2 (2007): 1–39.

Young, J. Michael. "Existence and Objectivity in Kant's Critique of Pure Reason." *Southwestern Journal of Philosophy* 9, no. 1 (1978): 61–68.

Zöller, Günter. "Critique of Pure Reason." *Philosophical Review* 111, no. 1 (2002): 113–116.

Zöller, Günter. "Main Developments in Recent Scholarship on the Critique of Pure Reason." *Philosophy and Phenomenological Research* 53, no. 2 (1993): 445–466.

INDEX

assertoric, as form of
judgment, 42
attractive and repulsive force,
laws of, 45

B

Berkeley, George, 36–37,
46–47

C

categorical, as form of
judgment, 42
categories of understanding,
18, 33, 39–40, 42
–43, 48
causality, 11, 45, 61
certainty, as one of five
requirements of
reason, 5
clarity, as one of five
requirements of
reason, 5
coexistence, principle of, 45
completeness, as one of five
requirements of reason, 5
concepts
intuitions and, 12, 13–
18, 57

as one of four necessary
elements of
experience, 19
contradiction, principle of, 9
Copernicus, 36, 47, 63
critique, use of term, 4
Critique of Judgment (Kant), ix
Critique of Practical Reason
(Kant), ix
critique of pure reason
metaphysics as related to, 6
motivation for, 35
Critique of Pure Reason (Kant)
A page numbers as from
1781 edition, xii
B page numbers as from
1787 edition, xii
Kant's reasons for, 5–6
known as first critique, ix
Norman Kemp Smith's
translation of, xii
primary aim of, x
reputation of, x

D

Descartes, René, 36–38, 45–47
dialectic, according to Kant,
51, 54

empirical judgments, 10

faculty of, 41

forms of, 33, 41–42

general logic as mere canon
of, 51

importance of, 7

a posteriori judgments, 8, 10

synthetic a priori
judgments, x, 1,
7–11, 12, 20, 26,
30, 36, 40, 52–
53, 59

K

knowledge

absolutely pure
knowledge, 4n4

as discursive, 7, 41

intuitions and concepts as
elements of, 57

Kant as changing reference
point of, 47

principle of all analytic
knowledge, 9

a priori knowledge, 10, 42

pure knowledge, 4n4, 53

synthetic a priori
knowledge, 31

Korsgaard, Christine M., 65

L

Leibniz, G. W., 36–37, 62

logic

applied general logic, 50

general logic, 33, 49–
53, 59

role of, 53

of special employment,
33, 49

transcendental analytic
logic, 53–54, 59

transcendental dialectic
logic, 53

transcendental logic, 33,
49, 51–53

logico-semantic distinction, 65

M

material atomism, 38

material idealism, 33, 36–38,
46–47, 61–62

mathematical principles,
48, 55

matter, definition of, 43

mechanics, laws of, 46

*Metaphysical Foundations
of Natural Science*
(Kant), 44

Printed in the United States
By Bookmasters